Junior Science
time

Terry Jennings

Illustrations by David Anstey

Gloucester Press
New York · London · Toronto · Sydney

About this book

You can learn many things about time in this book. It tells you about different objects used for measuring time and how they work. There are lots of activities and experiments for you to try. You will find out how to make sand, water and candle clocks, how to make a sundial and much more.

First published in the
United States in 1988 by
Gloucester Press
387 Park Avenue South
New York, NY 10016

ISBN 0 531 17112 4

Library of Congress Catalog
Card Number: 88-80394

© BLA Publishing Limited 1988

This book was designed and produced by BLA
Publishing Limited, TR House, Christopher
Road, East Grinstead, Sussex, England.
A member of the Ling Kee Group
London Hong Kong Taipei Singapore New York

Printed in Spain by Heraclio Fournier, S.A.

Think about what time you got up this morning and when you came to school. Now think about what time you have lunch and what time you will have supper. You can make a picture clock like this. It can show what time you do lots of different things.

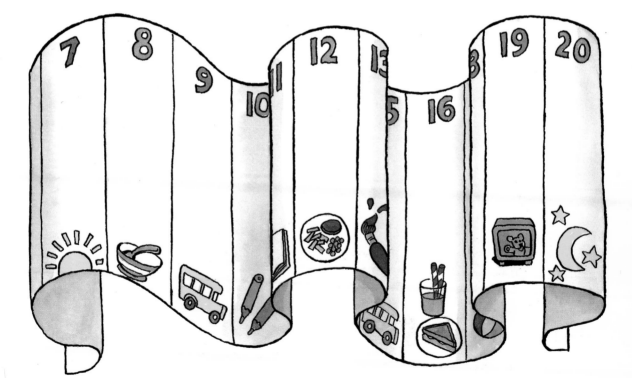

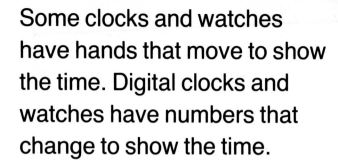

Some clocks and watches have hands that move to show the time. Digital clocks and watches have numbers that change to show the time.

Some clocks and watches are run by electricity which comes from a battery or plug in the wall. In other clocks and watches a spring moves the hands. From time to time the spring has to be wound up.

All of these objects measure time. Some work by springs and others use electricity.

4

Your shadow changes as time passes during the day. Look at your shadow early one sunny morning. Ask a friend to chalk around your feet and your shadow. The shadow will be long. At lunchtime stand in the same place and do this again. You will find that the shadow has moved and is much shorter. Later in the afternoon your shadow will have moved again and will be longer.

This is a sundial. Some large gardens and churches have sundials. A sundial can tell you the time on a sunny day. The pointer on the sundial makes a shadow when the sun shines. The shadow is in the same place at the same time each day.

You could make a sundial. First push a stick into the grass. At 9 o'clock look for the shadow of the stick. Mark the end of the shadow with a pebble. At 10 o'clock the shadow will have moved. Mark the end of the shadow with another pebble. If you mark the position of the shadow every hour, you can then use the stick as a sundial.

This is an egg timer. It has sand in it. An egg timer is really a sand clock. It tells you how long to boil an egg. When all the sand has run from the top to the bottom, the egg will be cooked.

Try making a sand clock. Ask a grown-up to cut the bottom off a plastic bottle.

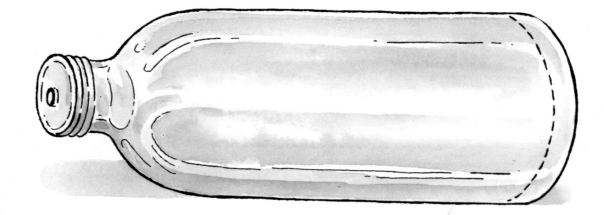

Mark some lines on a strip of paper and put it inside a jar. Stand the bottle in the jar. Fill the bottle with fine dry sand. Stand the bottle upside down over the jar. Count slowly until the sand gets to the first line. If you check your sand clock against another egg timer you can use it to time an egg.

9

You can make a water clock.
Take a plastic cup and make a
hole in the bottom with a pin.
Stand the cup on top of a jar
like this. Fill the cup with water.

Now count slowly until the
water reaches the first line on
the paper. Then count until the
water reaches the next line on
the paper. (The water will
reach the first line quicker
because the bottom of the jar
is rounded and holds less
water.) You can now time
some things with your clock.

You can make another water clock in a different way. Ask a grown-up to help. Nail together two pieces of wood like this. Find six plastic cups. Make a tiny hole in the bottom of five of them. Use thumb tacks to fix the cups to the upright piece of wood. Put the cup without a hole at the bottom.

Now fill the top cup with water. Using a watch with a second hand, see how long it takes for all the water to reach the bottom cup.

Make a candle clock. Measure a candle. Stand it up in plasticine in a metal tray. Ask a grown-up to light the candle for you. Let it burn for 10 minutes. Then blow the candle out and measure it again. You will then know how much of the candle will burn in 10 minutes.

Draw lines on the rest of the candle this distance apart. Put a pin in each of the lines. Ask a grown-up to light the candle again. When the candle has burned this distance the pin will drop out. The candle will burn for 10 minutes for each of the marks on it.

An alarm clock rings and wakes you up when it is time to get up in the morning. It rings at the time it is set to ring.

candle   pin   thread

plasticine

marble

This is a picture of a very strange alarm clock. When the candle burns down to the pin, the pin will fall out. Then the marble will fall with a clatter into the saucepan. Don't try to make this clock without the help of a grown-up!

All clocks and watches show hours and minutes. Some also show how many seconds have gone by. This clock has three hands. The red one is called a second hand. It shows how many seconds have gone by. It takes 60 seconds, or one minute, for the hand to go all the way around.

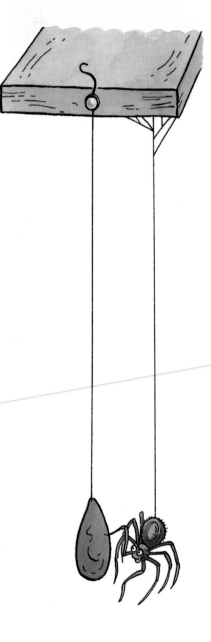

A pendulum is a wire or rod with a weight at the end that swings back and forth. You can make a pendulum. Tie a weight to a piece of string. Tie the string to a thumb tack in a piece of wood. Count how many times the pendulum swings back and forth in 10 seconds.

Now make the string longer and swing the pendulum again. It will swing fewer times in 10 seconds. Make the string still longer and it will swing fewer times again. But if you change the weight of the pendulum it will still swing at the same speed.

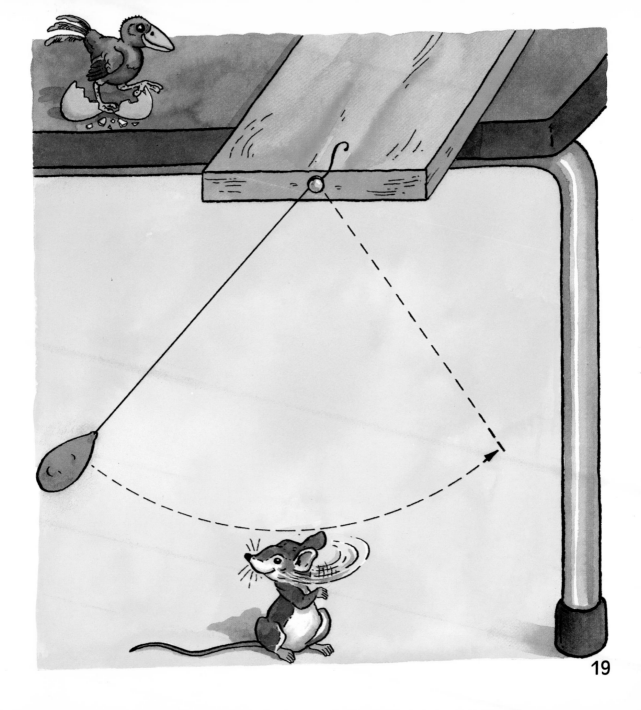

This is an old clock. It is called a grandfather clock. A pendulum makes the grandfather clock keep the correct time. The pendulum swings back and forth.

But the pendulum does not move on its own. The pendulum is moved by a heavy weight. The weight slowly falls as the pendulum swings. After a few days the weight has to be lifted up again. The weight is lifted by winding it up with a key.

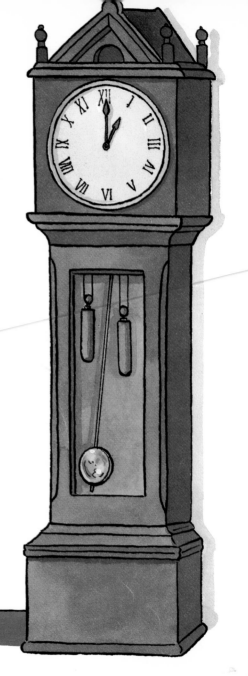

You can hear your heart beating if you do this.
Take a piece of rubber tube and two plastic
funnels. Fix the funnels to the tube as in the
picture. Put one funnel over your heart. Put the
other funnel to your ear. Now count how fast your
heart is beating. It may beat about 95 times a
minute. It will beat faster if you run!

bean seedling

Many plants seem to be able to tell the time. Every morning in summer daisies open. Then they close up every evening. Bean seedlings like the one in the picture change from morning to night. The leaves are held out during the day toward the sun. At night the leaves hang down.

glossary

Here are the meanings of some words you may have used for the first time in this book.

alarm clock: a clock that rings at the time you set it for.

battery: a device for storing and supplying electricity.

clock: an instrument for measuring and showing the passage of time.

egg timer: a sand clock that is used to show how long it takes to boil an egg.

pendulum: a swinging wire or rod with a weight on the end.

second: a unit of time. Sixty seconds make one minute.

seedling: a young plant.

shadow: the dark shape which appears on the ground or on a wall when an object is between it and the light.

spring: a springy device made of a coil of metal or wire.

sundial: a device that shows the time by a shadow cast by the sun.

index